The story of *The Nutcracker* is based on Alexandre Dumas' version of a fairy tale by the great German story teller, E. T. A. Hoffman. Featuring the familiar Tchaikovsky score, the first full-length ballet of *The Nutcracker* was presented on December 18, 1892 at the Maryinsky Theater in St. Petersburg. Boston Ballet mounted its first production of *The Nutcracker* in 1965. With an audience of more than 140,000 people, this production has become the most popular in the world.

Published by
Hare & Hatter Books, Inc.
15 Wykeham Road, West Newton, MA 02165

Design by Robert Segal

First Edition

10 9 8 7 6 5 4 3 2 1

Library of Congress Cataloging-in-Publication Data
The Nutcracker / Illustrated by Bud Rose; story retold by Jonathan McPhee and Suzanne Burakoff.
p. cm.
SUMMARY: A retelling of the story of Tchaikovsky's "The Nutcracker", based on the Boston Ballet production.
Preassigned LCCN: 96-78443
ISBN   0-9640792-1-6

1. Fairy tales--Juvenile literature. 2. Christmas--Juvenile fiction
3. Ballets--Stories, plots, etc.-- Juvenile literature.
I. Tchaikovsky, Peter Ilich, 1840-1893. Schelkunchik.
II. McPhee, Jonathan. III. Burakoff, Suzanne. IV. Rose, Bud.

PZ8.N95 1996   [E]
                                             QBI96-40454

BOSTON BALLET PRESENTS

THE NUTCRACKER

ILLUSTRATED BY BUD ROSE

story retold by
JONATHAN McPHEE
and SUZANNE BURAKOFF

Hare & Hatter Books
Newton MA

It is Christmas eve. Outside, a soft and silent snowfall covers the city. Inside, the Silberhaus family prepares for a grand celebration.

The Silberhaus children, Clara and Fritz, are filled with anticipation as the first guests arrive. All the children rush in to admire the table piled high with sweets. They guess at what secret surprises lie hidden in the boxes beneath the tree.

The party begins with everyone exchanging gifts and dancing. The room is filled with laughter and music and the sounds of children playing.

Suddenly Dr. Drosselmeyer, Clara's Godfather, arrives!

He has brought with him many magical presents:
life-sized dolls who dance,
a dancing bear,
and for Clara, his favorite niece, a very special Nutcracker.

In a moment of jealousy, her brother Fritz grabs
the Nutcracker from his sister and it breaks.

Clara sobs as Dr. Drosselmeyer does his best to mend the toy
by tying his handkerchief around the broken jaw.

After a final dance together, all of the guests leave and Clara's father carries a very sleepy daughter upstairs to bed.

The clock chimes twelve times, breaking the silence of the night. Little eyes seem to appear in every corner. A pattering of tiny feet is heard across the floor. *Mice* are everywhere!

Later that night, Clara awakes, worried about her precious Nutcracker. She tiptoes down the stairs to a dark, lonely living room. Mysterious things begin to happen all around her.

Suddenly Dr. Drosselmeyer has reappeared! Clara sees her Godfather working his magic as the room grows larger all around her. The walls go up and up . . . . And the tree! The tree grows so high she cannot see the top.

Now Clara's Nutcracker has grown tall as well.
He springs to life just as the evil Mouse King
and his army of mice approach.

The Nutcracker takes command. He bravely leads his toy soldiers into battle.

Trumpets blare. Weapons clash. Cannonballs fly.

The Mouse King captures Clara, but she pulls herself free,
and just as the mice are about to win, Clara throws her
slipper and knocks the Mouse King over.

The Nutcracker defeats his enemy and the battle is won.

As the mice scamper off in defeat, Clara sees her wooden Nutcracker transformed into a handsome prince!

He gently places a crown on Clara's head and leads her out into an enchanted forest.

Clara and her Prince are surrounded by snowflakes swirling and dancing in the moonlight. The Snow King and Queen come forward to greet them and lead them to a splendid balloon which will carry them to the magical Land of Sweets.

They leave the forest and sail through the sky over marzipan domes and lacy sugar towers. The Sugarplum Fairy greets them as they land in front of the dazzling Palace of Sweets.

Clara and her Prince are honored for their victory over the evil Mouse King. As they sit upon a throne in a room full of candy, they are entertained by dancers from many strange and wondrous lands.

The bright costumes and quick movements of the dancers from China delight them.

Next come the Russians in a dance called "Trepak." Looking like acrobats, they go faster and faster, higher and higher.

Mother Ginger enters with dozens of children scampering out from beneath her very wide skirts.

After the graceful Waltz of the Flowers, led by the glistening Dew Drop, the Sugarplum Fairy enters.

Finally it is time for the festivities to end with a beautiful dance by the Sugarplum Fairy and her Prince.

At last, waving good-by, Clara and the Nutcracker Prince get into their balloon, leaving the Land of Sweets behind, as they return home with memories of beautiful music and dreams of far away places.